TREASURES
of
AMERICAN
ARCHITECTURE

ACKNOWLEDGEMENTS

Special thanks to Joseph Ogrodnick for professional expertise in processing certain photographic prints. To Stephen O'Malley for assistance in handling equipment for special photographs.

ROSE HILL MANSION

This property has been designated a National Historic Landmark by the Secretary of the Interior in 1986. It has also been placed on the National Register of Historic Places.

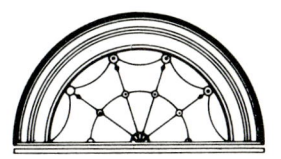

TREASURES of AMERICAN ARCHITECTURE

In Geneva, N.Y.

by
H. EDMOND WIRTZ

Photography by
DR. GEORGE J. HUCKER

Research by
ELEANORE R. CLISE, Archivist
Geneva Historical Society

Coordinated by
H. MERRILL ROENKE, JR.
Administrator and Curator
Rose Hill Mansion

Designed by
Louis H. Ferrini
Typography by
Marvin Flowers

Published by
THE GENEVA HISTORICAL SOCIETY
543 South Main Street
Geneva, New York 14456

Copyright © 1987 by The Geneva Historical Society

Reproduction in any manner, in whole or in part, in English
or in other languages is prohibited, unless permission
of the publisher is granted.

All Rights Reserved

First Published 1987

Library of Congress Catalog Card Number 87 - 80227.

International Standard Book Number ISBN 0-9613821-2-0

PRINTED IN THE UNITED STATES OF AMERICA
by Thomasson Printing Company
Carrollton, Georgia 30117

TABLE OF CONTENTS

Preface 6

How and Why Geneva Is As It Is 7

Map 9

Federal 1780-1820 11

Greek Revival 1820-1860 29

Gothic Revival 1840-1880 44

Italianate 1840-1885 55

Italian Villa 1830-1880 59

High Victorian Gothic 1860-1890 60

2nd Empire 1855-1885 67

Richardsonian Romanesque 1870-1900 70

Stick 1880-1890 77

Queen Anne 1880-1910 79

20th Century Innovations and Revivals 82

    Jacobean 1890-1940 84

    Tudor 1890-1940 87

    Prairie 1900-1920 89

    Sources .... (inside back cover)

PREFACE

Upstate New York is rich in architectural treasures; in few towns are those treasures so concentrated as they are in Geneva. It has enjoyed prosperity without suffering any explosive expansion, and its level of good taste has usually been high. The houses pictured here are, of course, the outstanding ones, but houses almost as good can be seen on almost every street. An architectural historian once said that our South Main Street is unique, but *North* Main Street would, in any less fortunate town, be considered a treasure too.

Though several well-known architects in New York City and in Rochester have designed buildings for Genevans, the local contractors were responsible for the greater part of the architecture here. In the present century there have been talented architects practicing in Geneva itself who have restored and embellished old buildings and have designed good new ones also. Our architectural preservation, thanks to the Historical Society, is becoming as good as our contruction.

This book should call our attention to buildings of which we were unaware, and should inspire us to maintain the high architectural standards which they exemplify.

Warren Hunting Smith

GENEVA ON SENECA LAKE

In this view from the east side of Seneca Lake showing Geneva on the west side, the houses of South Main Street, which stand on the ridge above the lake, can be seen among the trees.

WHY AND HOW GENEVA IS AS IT IS

Geneva is a small city in Western New York with remarkable architecture in a charming setting on Seneca Lake. The northwestern part of the city was the site of Kanadesaga, the capital of the Seneca nation of the Iroquois Confederacy. From here in 1779 Joseph Brant (Thayendanegea), War Chief of the Iroquois, led them and the British against the oncoming Sullivan-Clinton Expedition sent by General George Washington to break the power of the Indians and British. The tragic end came at the Battle of Newtown where the Indians were defeated and fled westward to the shores of Lake Erie and Canada.

The 5,000 soldiers in the Sullivan-Clinton Expedition had seen the immense agricultural resources of the Finger Lakes region. They had seen "neatly laid out gardens of peas, onions, squash, beans, parsnips, cabbage, cucumbers, watermelons, pumpkins, extensive fields of corn with ears twenty inches or more on stalks as high as eighteen feet," as well as great orchards of apples, pears, and peaches. Hence, the fine loam soil of Ontario County was the first great impetus to settlement and is still its major natural resource.

What is known chiefly about the log cabin stage of Geneva is that it soon vanished. The real founding of Geneva may be said to date from 1792 when Sir William Pulteney, 5th Baronet of Westerhall and Member of Parliament, bought 1,200,000 acres in Western New York from Robert Morris, "financier of the Revolution." Sir William was not only rich but also an experienced builder and developer. Geneva thus had a wealthy, aristocratic sponsor from its earliest days.

Sir William sent as his agent Captain Charles Williamson, a former British Army officer. In 1792 Captain Williamson, who is regarded as the real "founder" of Geneva, made his first visit to the Pulteney domain. In 1793 he completed laying out the village with its center a square, now Pulteney Park, on the high bluff overlooking the lake. A dynamo of energy, Captain Williamson proved to be a super developer. Armed with personal introductions from George Washington, he recruited settlers of a higher class than the usual pioneers. They came from New England, eastern New York, Pennsylvania, Maryland, and Virginia.

In 1796 Captain Williamson built the Geneva Hotel on the park at Sir William's expense. To manage this hostelry he imported Thomas Powell, a well-known British inn-keeper. Already Geneva was passing beyond the pioneer stage. By 1800 Captain Williamson had spent $1,374,470 (in dollars of the time) in promoting Geneva and the Genesee country. Since he had returned only $147,924, Sir William became worried about his huge investment and replaced him in 1800 with the more conservative Colonel Robert Troup. Nevertheless, the influence of Captain Williamson and his employer, who was willing to spend so much money on development, established Geneva as a community of distinction.

In the 19th Century money was made in Geneva, but money also came to Geneva. Rich merchants, bankers, farmers, lawyers, owners of foundries, iron works, and coal mines as well as retired sea captains, admirals, and generals came bringing means with them. The local wealth was largely the result of agriculture. The superior soil and abundant rain led to the production of nursery stock: shrubs, flowers, and fruit trees. In the late 19th Century hundreds of acres were devoted to this industry which exported its products throughout the United States. The Erie Canal and later the railroads provided the means of shipping the nursery stock, the grain, the fruit, and other agricultural products to the eastern seaboard. The profits from the local industries and the infusions of money from those who came to Geneva because of its beautiful location were responsible for the building of the houses of architectural merit.

In addition to its natural assets Geneva developed two noteworthy educational centers. The early citizens were greatly interested in education. As early as 1798 they had established the Geneva Academy. In 1822 the trustees of the Academy petitioned the New York State Board of Regents for a charter which would raise the status of the Academy to that of a college. A prime mover in the establishment of a college, The Right Reverend John Henry Hobart (1775-1830), Episcopal Bishop of the State of New York, selected a site for the college on South Main Street overlooking Seneca Lake. Here Geneva Hall was erected in the Federal style in 1822. By 1825 the trustees had raised the money required by the Board of Regents and Geneva College received its charter. To commemorate the founder of the college the name was changed from Geneva College to Hobart College in 1852. In 1906 William Smith, one of the prosperous nurserymen, gave a large endowment to found William Smith as a women's school coordinate with Hobart. In Geneva the colleges were created by the town, not the town by the colleges.

The second outstanding educational institution, the New York State Agricultural Experiment Station, was another result of the fine loam soil of the region. In 1881 after years of struggle by the New York State Agricultural Society and the Grange against the seed and fertilizer interests the station was established. Through the efforts of Robert Swan (1826-1890), owner of Rose Hill, the "Premium Farm of the Empire State," the Experiment Station was located in Geneva. Here distinguished scientists have developed great improvements in grape culture, fruit trees, food science, and livestock.

Over a period of nearly two hundred years Geneva grew slowly and then stopped. This blessing in disguise prevented the wholesale destruction which rapid growth brought to other cities, and this preserved the major part of Geneva's architectural heritage. The Geneva Historical Society has been energetic in promoting restoration and rehabilitation of houses and buildings which have suffered from alterations or neglect. In 1969 the Society succeeded in establishing two

Historic Districts which are now protected by law. *The New York Times* of December 15, 1985 said in an article on inns in Western New York, "The point of staying in Geneva is the serenity of water, sky, and trees." The *Times* should have added, "And enjoy the ambiance of one hundred and fifty years of beautiful American architecture."

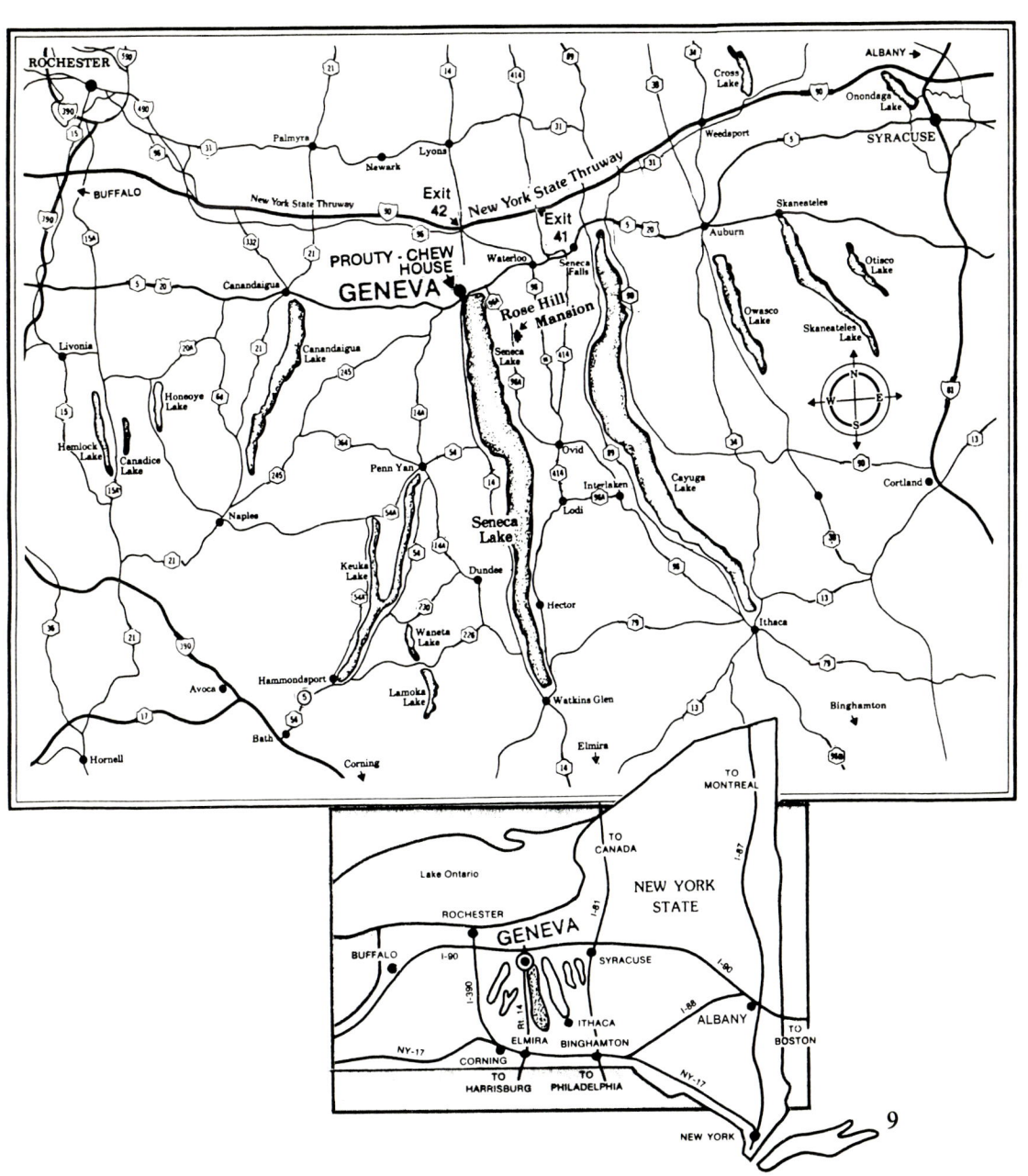

FEDERAL 1780-1820

The Federal style arose after the long reign of the Georgian house. The Adam brothers, Robert and James, were responsible for this style characterized by motifs of classical architecture modified into great lightness of proportion and extreme elegance. Since the spread of this style coincided with the establishment and early growth of the Federal government, it has long been called Federal. Modern critics prefer the nomenclature, "American phase of the English Adam style."

The dominant feature of the Federal house is the front door "surround"—a semi-elliptical fan-light over the door with delicate vertical side lights. Roofs are usually low-pitched with a cornice line balustrade. Double-hung sash windows with six panes over six are placed singly but in symmetrical rows. Chimneys may either be central with numerous flues for fireplaces in different rooms on different floors, or may be placed at the gable ends of the house.

Geneva's first growth coincided with the Federal period; hence, its first houses are in that style. Since the early plan of Geneva featured a village square (now Pulteney Park) laid out in 1793 at the direction of Captain Charles Williamson, the Pulteney land agent, the contiguous brick row houses in the Federal style surrounding the Park and adjacent South Main Street provide a unique example in Western New York of the Federal or Adamesque style.

WILLIAMSON HOUSE, 1829, 839 South Main Street

This splendid example of a free-standing Federal house was built by Charles A. Williamson, son of Captain Charles Williamson, agent and promoter for Sir William Pulteney Bt. and Associates. The cornice of a low-pitched roof is crowned with a parapet of solid panels and fretwork. The door "surround" has a well-proportioned elliptical fanlight with delicate side lights. Four chimneys are symmetrically placed. Flush board sheathing covers the front of the house. The windows are evenly spaced with six over six panes of glass. Many of these have the original greenish tinted glass. The porch, a later addition, has a parapet matching that on the roof. It was formerly on the wing to the right. A high styled example of the Federal mode, the house radiates spacious dignity.

HALLWAY OF SCOTT-REED HOUSE
A semi-elliptical fanlight with tracery in an Adamesque design artistically divides the hall. A finely scaled stairway at the rear ascends to the second floor.

SCOTT-REED HOUSE, 1815, 498 South Main Street
Unpretentious, and the only Geneva Federal house with the gable facing the street, the feature is the door surround of semi-elliptical fanlight with four side lights on each side. The gable is centered with a fanlight window. This house has a characteristically central chimney with several flues.

TROUP HOUSE, 1813, 98 Washington Street
  Colonel Robert Troup, land agent of the Pulteney Estate after the retirement of Captain Charles Williamson, built this house next to the Pulteney Land Office. A large Federal doorway with impressive surround of elegant colonettes of wood with glass lights centers the house.

PROUTY - CHEW HOUSE, 1829, 543 South Main Street
This is the home and museum of the Geneva Historical Society.
An outstanding Adam door and surround dominate this large house. Windows are evenly spaced with gray keystones in the lintels.

PULTENEY LAND OFFICE, 1824, West wing 1850, East wing 1908, 106 Washington Street

Native cut stone forms the central pavilion of this house. The doorway deeply set in the masonry has the Adam transom fanlight of the Federal period. The columns are smooth shaft Ionic with volutes at 45° angles.

FOLGER HOUSE, 1831, 105 Jay Street
  The raised basement of this house distinguishes it from other Federal houses. The door, off-center, has a semi-elliptical fanlight. The prevalence of the round arch in the Federal style is also seen in the entrance to the basement. A low hipped roof completes the silhouette of the house.

TRINITY RECTORY, 1810, 528 South Main Street

Striking in this house is the balustraded deck on the hip roof. End view shows a fanlight window at the top, a full rounded window in the center, and two one-quarter fanlights on either side. Three dormer windows project through the roof. The front of the house has tongue and groove siding with Adam moldings over the windows. The wing has a small porch with slender Ionic columns. The door has a transom with full-length side lights.

HAVILAND HOUSE, c. 1840, 30 Geneva Street

A gem of a house, this brick dwelling has chimneys in each gable. The windows are distinguished by sashes of twelve panes each. The porch with Ionic columns fronts a door with handsome transom and three-quarter-length side lights. On the right side, not shown, is an Adam elliptical window which illuminates the hall.

SCHERMERHORN-deLANCEY HOUSE, 1826, 616 South Main Street
   A sturdy brick example of the Federal style, the house has a one-story porch with slender Doric columns. This house was for many years the home of William Heathcote deLancey (1797-1865), first Bishop of Western New York (1838).

GENEVA HALL, 1822, HOBART COLLEGE, South Main Street

A relatively large but simple Federal building, the masonry of Geneva Hall is of solid cut stone from a local source. The lintels, sills, and corner quoins are of a lighter colored stone than the walls. The building displays three typical "beltings" of the period. Placed on a site selected by Bishop John Henry Hobart (1775-1830) for whom the college was later named, the structure has been in continuous use since its opening in 1822.

RUMNEY - STODDARD HOUSE, 1808, rebuilt 1830, 606 South Main Street
   Basically a simple Federal house, it was destroyed by fire in 1830 and rebuilt. The classical porch with balustrade on the roof and the Palladian window over it are later additions.

SCHERMERHORN HOUSE, 1827, 584 South Main Street
  Ionic columns with smooth shafts topped with volutes at 45° angles support a narrow entablature with dentils. The pediment has a semi-elliptical window and dentils on the cornice. Full-length windows on the ground floor give on to double parlors which occupy the front of the house.

PORCH AND ENTRYWAY OF SCHERMERHORN HOUSE
  Smooth Ionic columns with volutes at 45° angles support a roof with dentil molding on the cornice. The door has a transom and three-quarter sidelights with delicate and elegant Adam tracery.

FEDERAL ROW HOUSES, 490, 492, and 496 South Main Street, built 1808-1820
The first house on the left is a large four bay house with dentil molding under the cornice and a cornice line balustrade above. A carriageway on the right led to stables in the rear. The others in the row are of varying heights with classical porches added.

LUDLOW HOUSE AND ADJACENT ROW HOUSES, 1820, 388, 394, 400, and 402 South Main Street

The Ludlow house shows a panelled cornice line parapet. The windows have twelve panes over twelve. The white trim under the cornice and around the door and windows is simple but elegant. The early style of the house is reflected in the large centered chimney.

Adjacent is the beginning of a series of row houses both wood and brick. The carriageway under the second house provided access to stables and barns in the rear.

SUTHERLAND HOUSE, 1821, 56 Park Place
  This fine example of a Federal Row House facing Pulteney Park has a discrepancy in design in that the two windows on the left were part of the house next door which was annexed in later years. The 20th Century entry porch with a curved underside of the roof conforms to the Federal doorway.

WHITE-WILSON TAVERN, KANADESAGA CLUB, 1831,
485-487 South Main Street

This large three-story brick structure is attractive for its scale and symmetry. The front and side doors are large with elaborate door surrounds of transom and side lights of glass in lead tracery. Four chimneys terminate the low pitched roof.

FEDERAL MANTEL

This Adamesque mantelpiece is typical of mantels in Federal houses in Geneva. Vase-shaped pilasters support the entablature and shelf. The mantel is in the former Bank of Geneva building of 1831, now the Geneva Woman's Club. The portriat by Louise Newton Reed is of Agnes Bevan Lewis, first president of the Woman's club, 1918.

Greek Revival 1820-1860

Guided by the impetus for classical styled buildings which came from the leadership of George Washington and Thomas Jefferson in selecting the design for the first public buildings in Washington, the new Republic of the United States looked back to democratic Athens and republican Rome for inspiration. The style of the Greek temple became the pattern for houses, banks, schools, churches, and sundry other buildings. Doric, Ionic, or Corinthian columns upheld the front gable of houses facing the street. The semi-elliptical fanlight over the main door with side lights of the Federal house disappeared in favor of the rectangular door "surrounded" with rectangular panes held in a delicate frame. Houses without full height columns sometimes have pilasters and always have the deep cornice or entablature of the Greek temple.

Sometimes called the "National Style," the aesthetic of the Greek Revival was balance, dignity, coolness, and formality.

VAN BRUNT-FOOTE HOUSE, 1835, 1847, 46 Delancey Drive
　A Doric portico of great strength and simplicity dignifies this very large mansion with two equal-sized wings. A triangular window in the center of the pediment punctuates its triangular shape.

SEELYE HOUSE, 1848, 140 Genesee Street
   A story and one-half in the front, four Ionic columns support a well-proportioned entablature and pediment. The front wall is tongue and groove to provide a flat surface for the play of light and shadow. Four pilasters on the wall strengthen it. The door is recessed behind two small Ionic columns and surrounded with transom and side lights. Windows in the frieze band have cast iron decorative gratings. The house quietly proclaims its unique character.

VAN GIESON HOUSE, 1840, 273 Washington Street

A deep entablature with dentil molding at the top surrounds the house and is supported at the front by Ionic columns. Unusual is the lack of a pediment over the columns. Windows on the front are floor length; second story windows protrude into the entablature which also has frieze band windows with decorative iron gratings. A simple entry porch on the side has Ionic columns and pilasters. The doorway is recessed and is surrounded with transom and side lights.

LEWIS HOUSE (on the left), 1848, 96 Pulteney Street and
MESSUR HOUSE (on the right), 1850, 92 Pulteney Street
  These brick dwellings are a finely matched pair, both with wings on the left side. The Lewis house has Doric columns, and the Messur house Ionic.

HOPGOOD HOUSE, 1840, 128 Washington Street

A perfect example of a five bay brick Greek Revival house whose gable end does not face the street, this dwelling has a one story entry porch with Doric columns and pediment centered in the front of the house. A deep entablature stretches across the front and wraps around the ends. The symmetry and scale of this house are outstanding.

SIMPSON HOUSE, 1841, 5 Genesee Park

Nicely scaled, this house has four Ionic columns full height and four smaller columns on the wing. The door is recessed with pilasters on each side with transom and side lights. Windows are topped with miniature pediments.

DITMARS HOUSE, 1852, 218 Washington Street
  This fine example of a "vernacular" Greek Revival house shows three columns instead of an even number and they are square rather like "antae." A narrow door has transom only, while a fanlight window is centered in the pediment.

MITCHELL HOUSE, 1839, 152 Genesee Street
This charming red brick house with four Ionic columns plus two smaller columns on the wing is beautifully proportioned. The over-scaled door with pilasters on the sides is recessed with transom and side lights. Lintels and sills of windows are cut limestone. First floor windows are full length.

WATSON - CHEW HOUSE, 1838, 600 South Main Street

The "monumental" full-length colonnade of four Ionic columns which fronts the house is of a scale with the remainder of the house. A semi-elliptical fanlight window centers the impressive pediment. Windows of the first floor front are floor length and illuminate double parlors. All windows are finished with heavy limestone lintels and sills. The main entrance in the center of the left side has a small porch with Ionic columns and a door surround of transom and side lights.

CLARK HOUSE, 1820, 859 South Main Street
This original brick Federal house was converted to Greek Revival which explains the unusual width of the Ionic portico. The elliptical window in the side wall is a Federal characteristic. The door surround of transom and side lights is Greek Revival.

ROSE HILL, 1838, Rte. 96 A

An apogee of Greek Revival architecture in Geneva and Western New York was reached in the building of this mansion in 1838 by Brigadier General William Kerley Strong. A "monumental" colonnade of six Ionic columns fronts the main pavilion with recessed wings on either side having two Ionic columns. Measurements of the main columns are close to those of the Erechtheum in ancient Athens, but the pediment is higher, suggesting Roman power. The entire mass is crowned with a cupola of stylized Greek design, a typical feature of New York State Greek Revival architecture.

The front door, centered in the portico, is recessed within two free-standing Ionic columns flanked by two pilasters supporting an entablature with leaf and tongue carving and the bead and reel of the Erechtheum. The door is surrounded with transom lights and the inner section is outlined with egg-and-dart molding in bold relief.

Through the generosity of Waldo Hutchins, Jr., this house was restored and given to the Geneva Historical Society. The interior has American Empire furnishings and decorations. The house is open to the public from May 1 through October 31st.

REAR VIEW OF ROSE HILL

The pavilion or main block of the house with its impressive portico and the two lower and recessed wings, also with Ionic columns, form a sculptural entity composed of three geometric solids. A fourth volume is the three dimensional negative space of the courtyard lying between the wings at the rear of the building. In this courtyard, the rear of the pavilion displays upper and lower porches with square columns or posts. Both porches are enclosed by ornamental railings in the sheaf of wheat design. They do not permit entrance from the outside, but rather furnish passages from one wing of the house to the other without entering the main pavilion. The wing on the left, formerly the wood house, is now an open roofed terrace. The wing on the right houses the kitchen, which is part of the original Robert Rose house built in 1809.

FRONT PARLOR OF ROSE HILL

The Front Parlor features an eight piece Classic Rococco Revival parlor set in rosewood, 1845, by Alexander Roux of New York City (1837-1881). Roux was a master French cabinet maker/*ebeniste*, who created the "most graceful and elaborate works" of the period. Unlike the furniture of John H. Belter (1804-1861), the Roux furniture is solid rosewood, not laminated, is less flamboyant and more refined. This set of eight pieces shows Roux at his best. "The naturalism of the floral carving is an astonishing accomplishment" since rosewood is very difficult to work with because of its grain and resinous nature. Between the windows, which are hung with an Italian silk damask in an Empire design, is a pastel portrait of Agnes Swan Hutchins by J.W. Champney (1843-1903), date 1900. Under the portrait is a mahogany Empire card table with gold leaf banding and carved claw feet with acanthus leaves. This is a piece of the original Swan furniture. On the table is a three branch Empire ormulu girandole of a Roman soldier with cut glass prisms. In the center of the room is a round mahogany Empire pedestal table with marble top and gold leaf trim. On the white marble mantel, which has slender pilasters, is a pair of double Argand lamps with original frosted and cut glass shades in the Gothic style by John B. Jones, Boston, Massachusetts. Centered is an early sage green Wedgwood bowl. Above the mantel is a fine 17th Century Flemish painting of a landscape with stag hunt scene, signed Gillis Neyts (1623-1687), dated 1653.

THE BANQUET ROOM OF ROSE HILL

Quite the largest and most impressive room in the mansion is the Banquet Room 29 feet 8 inches long and 21 feet 4 inches wide. The wallpaper is a Nancy McClelland reproduction of a French Empire paper. The windows are hung with embroidered curtains completed with blue silk tasseled valances in tambour style. The mahogany American Sheraton banquet table supported by reeded legs has demi-lune ends with large floor length drop leaves. The table is set with an English dessert service of the Empire period centered by a Sheffield epergne, c. 1800, fitted with cut glass. The mahogany chairs with leather seats are a set of twelve (two arm chairs and ten side), in the transitional style of the 1840's which were part of the Swan furnishings. Over the table hangs a Portuguese crystal chandelier of 1815 with cut glass prisms. The fireplace centered in the outside wall has a mantel with pilasters derived from the ancient Tower of the Winds in Athens as illustrated by Stuart and Revett in *The Antiquities of Athens* (1762-1816). Over the mantel is a large convex mirror framed in gold leaf. On the mantel is a pair of Sevres vases in cobalt blue, gold and floral decoration. On either side is a pair of pierced ladderback Chippendale chairs which were brought to Rose Hill in 1803 by Robert Rose.

The Empire pier table between the windows was made by Haines and Holmes, (1826-1830), in New York City. White marble columns with ormulu capitals uphold a marble top. The carved claw feet are "antique vert" which was a method of simulating ancient bronze by using a deep green-black paint highlighted with powdered gold to enhance the effect of burnishing. The apron is decorated with gold leaf stencilling and banding. On the table is a Sheffield hot water urn, formerly the property of Moses Rogers of New York City. Flanking it is a pair of Chinese Export garnitures decorated with the American eagle and foo dogs on top. Over the table is a Federal gilt mirror. On the sideboard is a five piece silver coffee and tea service made by I.W. Forbes of New York City in 1816. The service was a wedding present to Benjamin and Mary Saidler Swan and was inherited by their son Robert. The service was returned to Rose Hill by Benjamin Swan's great-great grandson, Waldo Hutchins III.

Over the sideboard is an exceptionally large still life painting of fruits, c. 1850, by Severin Roesen, (W. in America 1848-1871). This hangs exactly where it hung during the Swan years.

Gothic Revival 1840-1880

By 1840 the immense vogue of the Greek Revival began to wane. Alexander Jackson Davis championed Gothic buildings in his book *Rural Residences*. However, the style was really popularized by his friend Andrew Jackson Downing (1815-1852) in two books *Cottage Residences*, 1842, and *The Architecture of Country Houses*, 1850. Downing was a prophet with honor in his own land since his books went through many editions, mainly after his early death at age thirty-seven. A passenger on the Hudson River steamer *Henry Clay*, which caught fire while racing another ship and sank, Downing, after rescuing several passengers, himself drowned.

Downing wrote that "good" houses were necessary, "because a good house is a powerful means of civilization." His Rural Gothic Cottages were designed to free the builders from the strictures of the square or rectangular shape of the Greek Revival.

These Gothic Revival houses are easily recognizable from their high steeply pitched roofs and high pointed gables with decorative vergeboards in Gothicized style. Windows may be in the shape of the pointed Gothic arch or the flattened Tudor arch. A crown over the windows called a "drip mold" was both decorative and functional as a means of diverting water from running down on the window. Brick, stone, wood, or "unburnt" bricks were the construction materials. Downing gave specific instructions for building a house of "unburnt" or "sun dried bricks," now usually called "adobe." The bricks should be made either of clay or good loam soil mixed with straw. They should be one foot six inches long, six inches wide, and four inches thick. He directed the drying as follows: "Lay the bricks on level ground; turn them on the other edge on the second day. After three days of clear weather they will be dry enough to pile up under cover. There they should lie for a fortnight; then they will be ready to use." The outside wall of an adobe house should be plastered "with good lime mortar mixed with hair, and then a second coat of pebble dashed as in 'rough cast' walls." In addition to being less expensive than burned bricks, walls of unburnt brick absorb dampness less. A number of Geneva's Gothic Revival houses were constructed in this manner.

The scale of these houses was small as befits their designation as "cottages" and as Downing wrote ". . . would not require servants." Their essential line was vertical; their aesthetic appeal was to "picturesqueness" in reaction to the formality of the Greek Revival.

SILL HOUSE, 1845, 247 Washington Street
   Built of "unburnt" or adobe bricks, this cottage gets its smooth appearance from stucco over the bricks. The gables are lined with curvilinear vergeboards. The porch has Tudor arches between the supports.

BRADFORD HOUSE, 1850, 629 South Main Street
  Three asymmetrical gables with curvilinear vergeboards distinguish this cottage built of "unburnt" or adobe bricks. Windows have "drip molds" over them and leaded glass panes. The porch is decorated with crenelations along its roof line and flattened arches between its supports.

IRVING HOUSE, 1845, 731 South Main Street
Originally a Gothic cottage of "unburnt" brick covered with stucco, this house was enlarged and changed to resemble Spanish colonial. The gables and double chimneys attest to its Gothic beginning.

BALMANNO COTTAGE, 1830, 583 South Main Street
   Here is a quintessential example of a brick Downing Rural Gothic Cottage: Steeply pitched roofs are edged with deep many pointed vergeboards. The front gable topped by a finial shows a pointed arch Gothic window. Other windows have flattened arches. Dormer windows project through the roof. The aesthetic effect is charm and "picturesqueness."

ST PETER'S MEMORIAL CHURCH, 1868, Tower, 1878, Genesee Street

This church, built of cut red Medina sandstone and gray Lockport limestone, is rather a greatly enlarged chapel in the English Gothic style with perpendicular buttresses. The height of the building is developed from the very steep roof line. A large rose window is centered in the facade over the entry porch. The most unusual feature is the functionally detached massive tower with its main pointed spire surrounded by lesser spires. The tower contains the only carillon in Geneva.

In 1986 the accretions to the interior of the past one hundred years were swept away and the interior restored to its original Victorian Gothic appearance.

The church was erected as a memorial to The Right Reverend William Heathcote deLancey (1797-1865), first Bishop of Western New York. Bishop deLancey is buried beneath the high altar.

Architect of the church: Richard Upjohn, 1802-1878.
Architect of the tower: Richard M. Upjohn, 1828-1903.

HIPPLE HOUSE, 1850, 73 Genesee Street
   A small, double-gabled house with Gothic vergeboards, this dwelling has elaborate "drip molds" over each window.

LOVE HOUSE, 1872, 165 Washington Street

Although a brick Gothic cottage, with slate roof, this house has rounded stone arches over the windows. The many gables and tall chimneys emphasize its verticality. The porch, without railings, has flattened arches between the porch supports.

MT. CALVARY CHURCH OF GOD IN CHRIST, 1876, 21 Milton Street
　　The only surviving wooden church edifice in Geneva, this is by its simple but elegant design a fine example of wooden Gothic. The square tower with its graceful semi-broach spire dominates the church. Windows and main door are fully rounded with overhanging trim.

TRINITY CHURCH, 1844, restored in 1932 after a disastrous fire, South Main Street

Although Calvin Otis was the nominal architect, Trinity Church was largely the work of the Reverend Benjamin Hale (1797-1863), President of Hobart College, with a heavy leaning on Richard Upjohn (1802-1878), architect of Trinity Church in New York City.

Trinity Church, Geneva is a fine example of English perpendicular Gothic. The solid masonry construction is of coursed cut gray limestone. Perpendicular buttresses support the first floor walls and the clerestory. The tower is square in the manner of English country churches with the main entrance through the tower. Large Gothic windows with diamond shaped panes of glass illuminate the interior.

The chancel, added in 1898, has random ashlar limestone masonry. The mosaic pavement of the chancel, laid by Italian artisans, survived the fire. The chancel is illuminated by a great Gothic stained glass window over the high altar.

Below the high altar lies buried The Right Reverend Arthur Cleveland Coxe (1818-1896), second Bishop of Western New York.

Italianate 1840-1885

Andrew Jackson Downing is again responsible for popularizing this style derived from Italian farm houses, principally from the hills of Tuscany. Square or rectangular box-shaped, the Italianate house is easily identified by its low-hipped roof with two to four feet wide overhanging eaves heavily "bracketed," a term invented by Downing. The purposes of these overhangs were to convey a feeling of power, to cast deep and broad shadows, and to protect from sun and rain. The roof may be crowned with a cubicular cupola. Windows of the parlors usually extend to the floor and open on a narrow Italian veranda. The window openings may be rounded at the top with decorative enframements. A wing at the rear sometimes produces an L-shaped house. Solidity and spaciousness with a hint of grandeur are the chief artistic effects of the Italianate house.

ROENKE HOUSE, 1873, 112 William Street

Geneva abounds with Italianate houses, but most have had "improvements" such as new and different porches, raised roofs, changed windows. This house is prototypical and is in its original condition with its cupola, wide overhanging eaves, and porch of vague Renaissance design.

DENTON HOUSE, 1856, (PARROT HALL OF THE NEW YORK STATE AGRICULTURAL EXPERIMENT STATION) 643 West North Street

This immense five bay house of three stories exhibits wide overhanging eaves supported by very large paired brackets. Windows are rectangular with decorative crowns in a Renaissance design. An outstanding feature of the house is a wide porch of cast iron columns, railings, and roof line balustrade which surrounds the house on three sides.

THOMAS SMITH HOUSE, 1861, 546 Castle Street

Very broad eaves with brackets overhang this large, square house. The low pitched roof is crowned with a cubicular cupola. Windows are segmentally rounded or are paired fully rounded with a pedimented hood.

WILLIAM HENRY SMITH-THEODORE SMITH HOUSE, 1876, 534 Castle Street
   A four story square tower capped with a sharply pitched roof with pointed dormer window interjections centers this imposing example of an Italian villa. Asymmetrically placed wings with gables grouped around the tower have wide eaves with brackets. The front facing wing is dominated by a large bay of windows. Above this is a narrow wooden balcony with a roof. A front porch nestles between the base of the tower and the rear wing. The house fulfills Andrew Jackson Downing's requirements for "refinement and gracious living."
   Architects: Cutler and Warner of Rochester, New York.

DUNNING HOUSE, 1869, 25 Genesee Park
   This essentially flat-top house with flat-topped tower of great scale is genuinely Tuscan in spirit. Windows are tall with decorative hoods. Cast iron balustrades decorate the roof of both tower and house. The Eastlake style porch is a later addition.

Italian Villa 1830-1880

More ornate and irregular in shape than the Italianate house, the Italian villa is distinguished by a tower that is one or more stories taller than the remainder of the house. The tower is the focal point which establishes the beauty of proportion of the wings, gables, and porches. The roofs are low pitched with overhanging eaves or massive cornices. Windows are of various forms frequently topped by the Romanesque arch crowned with decorative stone.

Andrew Jackson Downing wrote that the main floor of villas should have a ceiling from twelve to fourteen feet in height and should have "never less than three or four apartments, i.e., drawing room, dining room, library, bedroom or office for the master," plus front and back stairs, kitchen, pantry, closets, etc. Italian villas should be the size that "requires three or more servants," he ordered. The Italian villa speaks of refinement, gracious living, and elegance.

High Victorian Gothic 1860-1890

High Victorian Gothic is a larger, more florid, more decorated incarnation of the Gothic mode than the earlier "cottages" of the Gothic Revival. Steep gables and steep pointed dormer windows projecting through the roof line are trimmed with heavier, deeper vergeboards. Both gables and dormer windows show a straight beam truss across them, forming a triangle. Frequently materials of different colors and textures create decorative banding or window crowns and trim. The architects of this style revelled in asymmetrical balancing of gables and wings, sharp contrasts, and enlarged "picturesqueness" to achieve an artistic lavishness which stimulated wonder and pride.

WRIGHT HOUSE, 1872, 223 North Street

This double gabled house with gabled dormer windows has restrained vergeboards with cross bracing and Gothic iron finials. Windows have segmented arched crowns. Second story cast iron balconies and open veranda with cast iron railings are unusual characteristics. The large main doorway with high transom, side lights, and pilasters is the important center of the house.

J.W. SMITH-DOVE HOUSE, 1872, 512 South Main Street

The great two-story porch with high gable, cross bracing, and finial is this house's exuberant attention-getting feature and an ultimate expression of High Victorian fantasy. Symmetrical gabled windows with vergeboards, cross bracing, and finials flank the porch. Multiple chimneys punctuate the steep roof. Segmentally shaped drip molds crown the windows. Altogether this house satisfied the High Victorian love of lavish "picturesqueness."

BLACKWELL HOUSE, 1861, William Smith Campus

A dual-pitched hip roof of slate shingles inset with sharply pointed dormer windows which have cross-bracing distinguishes this High Victorian mansion. Windows are arched in shape with Gothic pointed lintels. In addition, horizontal bands of varicolored brick establish a polychrome effect. A one story porch with roof supported by posts joined by flattened Tudor arches sweeps across the front. The increase in color and ornamentation shows the progression from the earlier Gothic Revival.

Architect: Richard Upjohn, 1802-1878. This is the first of a number of Upjohn buildings in Geneva.

ASHCROFT, 1862, 112 Jay Street
CENTER WING OF ASHCROFT

As an early example of the High Victorian Gothic style this brick house is outstanding. A version of the enlarged cottage, Ashcroft has multiple asymmetrical steep gables trimmed with deep elaborate vergeboards. The central wing has a three-sided bay window above which is a double window with hood. The large gable above has a double window whose stone lintels are fully rounded. The gable is surmounted by a small square tower of Gothic design finished with a steep spire. On the right is a porch with flattened Tudor arches between the posts. This once faced a formal boxwood garden.

LEFT WING OF ASHCROFT

The main entrance to the house is through a porch which has flattened Tudor arches and a balustraded roof above the entryway. Above it is a dormer window with deep vergeboards. Adjacent to the left is another gable with deep vergeboards. Further left is a very large gable similar to the front gable in size. It also has a three-sided bay on the first floor. An open veranda with balustrade encircles the side. Tudoresque chimneys pierce the roof. As an expression of high-styled Victorian Gothic, Ashcroft is hard to excel.

Architect: Calvert Vaux (1824-1895).

Note: In 1884 when President Chester A. Arthur came to Geneva to attend the funeral of his Secretary of the Treasury, Charles J. Folger of Geneva, he stayed at Ashcroft.

MOORE HOUSE, 1853, 760 Castle Street

The 19th Century saw numerous experiments in architecture such as Egyptian, Moorish, and other exotic conceptions. One of these, which is distinctly American, is the Octagon House. The style was originated by Professor Orson S. Fowler, a noted phrenologist of Fishkill, New York. Fowler claimed that an octagon encloses more space per linear foot of exterior wall than the usual square or rectangle, thereby "reducing building costs and heat loss through the wall." He also claimed "increasing sunlight and ventilation."

The Moore House shows two stories above a raised basement, thick brick walls, low-pitched hip roof, and wide eaves supported by pairs of Italianate brackets. The octagonal cupola illuminates the stairway in the center of the house. Windows with pediments over them are paired and centered in each of the eight sides. The doorway is Greek Revival with transom and sidelights. The house is made truly notable by a porch encircling the building. Columns, railings, and balustrades on its roof are of ornamental cast iron brought as ballast from Italy.

2nd Empire 1855-1885

When Louis Napoleon Bonaparte was proclaimed Emperor Napoleon III, the 2nd Empire was launched on its eighteen year career. The Emperor immediately began a massive reconstruction of Paris; and under the leadership of his brilliant director of public works, Baron Georges Eugene Haussmann, the Paris of the grand boulevards and vistas we see today was created.

The architecture of this 2nd Empire reflected the spirit of the regime—opulence, ostentation, extravagance, and richness of taste verging on vulgarity were its hallmarks. This new style immediately spread to Europe and the United States. The unmistakable feature of 2nd Empire buildings is the mansard roof (from Francois Mansart, 17th century architect to Louis XIV), with dormer windows on the steep lower slope. Cornices supported by ornamental brackets bind the roof of the house. Windows are frequently arched and paired with decorative wood or stone. Main entry doors are paired. Bay windows, asymmetrical porches, and porte-cochères complete the impression of lavishness. Among the great public buildings in the United States constructed in this style are the old Executive Office Building in Washington, D.C., erected during the administration of President U.S. Grant (1868-1876), and the City Hall of Philadelphia.

AFFLECK-NESTER HOUSE, 1865, 53 Genesee Street

As a triumph of opulence, the Affleck-Nester house is a paradigm of 2nd Empire richness. Here we have a concave mansard roof pierced with double windows heavily hooded with "S" scrolls at the base, a solid cornice with brackets binding the roof to the house, double windows with three white keystones and white stone sills. The four-story tower with mansard roof pierced with windows is embraced between two wings of the house. The combined rectangular and round porch, full length windows in a two-story bay, and a columned porte-cochère at the side complete a delicious panoply of ostentatious extravagance.

DAVID MOORE HOUSE, 1872, 57 High Street

This more restrained example of the 2nd Empire style has a straight mansard roof pierced by heavily hooded windows supported by a bracketed cornice. The windows of the first and second floors have segmentally arched tops. The asymmetrically placed bay windows on the front and side have bracketed cornices. The side ends with an important brick arch. The large hood over the double front door is supported by Renaissance brackets. This house, though large and imposing, is friendly and comfortable.

Richardsonian Romanesque 1870-1900

Henry Hobson Richardson (1838-1886) in the words of Lewis Mumford was "... a colossal man, an architect who almost singlehandedly created out of a confusion which was actually worse than a mere void the beginnings of a new architecture." The second American to graduate from the Ècole des Beaux Arts in Paris (Richard Morris Hunt being the first), Richardson worked his way first through Victorian Gothic; but then, instead of adopting the Neo-Renaissance style that began to be favored by other architects, he felt his way back further to the Southern French Romanesque from the 9th through the 12th centuries.

This style Richardson adapted and reinterpreted with great vigor. Trinity Church, Boston, built in this style, may be called his "signature" building; but he built and designed other churches, schools, libraries, warehouses, jails, railroad stations, city halls, bridges, and houses. The hallmarks of a Richardsonian building are massive masonry construction of cut stone and brick, the Romanesque or Syrian arch as an essential feature, round or polygonal towers, windows deeply recessed in the masonry. The purely decorative is minimal; the bulk and asymmetrical sculpted shapes of the buildings give them their great artistic individuality. They reflect his aesthetic concept that the structure must be designed from inside out, i.e., the function must determine the form.

Although he had "... the build and driving force of a bison," Richardson, at the height of his career, died prematurely in 1886 of Bright's disease. Nevertheless, in 1888 a monograph on his life and art by the art critic Mrs. Schuyler Van Rensselaer greatly stimulated his followers to continue the Richardsonian style.

Richardsonian buildings are always very expensive, architect designed, and of landmark quality. Although he was called a reformer, and an initiator, he was also "... the last traditional architect. Dying when he did, his architecture remained entirely within the historic past of traditional masonry."

ELKS CLUB, 1892, 459 South Main Street
   Built as the Collins Music Hall, this has been the club house of the Elks since 1908. More symmetry is displayed in this building than in the usual Richardson edifice. The centered arch with double doors is flanked by two arched windows with stained glass ellipses. Three large wall dormers with arches over them project from the steeply pitched roof. The solid masonry construction is a combination of brick and sandstone. The "music hall," which occupies the upper part of the building, has a barrel ceiling with Adam decoration. This rugged building demonstrates the adaptability of the Richardsonian style to different uses.

BELHURST, 1889, Lochland Road

All of the hallmarks of the Richardsonian style are encompassed in this magnificent house. Of solid masonry construction the walls are coursed local red Medina sandstone. (Richardson enthusiastically used a native stone if it were available.) The large porte-cochère arch supported by the cushioned capitals of short columns establishes the Romanesque character of the edifice. Two towers of different heights, one round, the other polygonal, dominate the sculpted shape of the house along with the steeply pitched roof of slate shingles. Windows are deeply recessed while chimneys emphasize the height of the house.

INTERIOR OF BELHURST

The interior arrangement follows Richardson's dictum that function should determine form. Traversing the length of the building is a great "living" hall with fireplace and a stairway which "cascades" in landings downward. The round arch fireplace surround echoes the arch of the porte-cochère. Brilliant mosaic work accentuates the dark wood around it. Grouped on the lake side for the view are the public rooms: library, morning room, drawing room, and solarium. Dining room, kitchen and service rooms occupy the land side. A lavish use of exotic woods such as white oak, quarter cut cherry, Honduras white mahogany establish an unexpected atmosphere of great warmth and livability.

Architect: Albert W. Fuller.

Photo by Joseph M. Ogrodnick

NEW YORK STATE ARMORY, 1893, 1907, 300 Main Street

A large, massive Richardsonian building of rusticated sandstone and brick, the Armory is centered by the heavy stone arch of the porch entryway. Two castellated towers, one round and one polygonal, asymmetrically placed, dominate the building. Both have narrow, deeply recessed windows and crenelated parapets at the top. Eight great recessed arches within which are narrow windows march across the entire facade. Although bold and fortress-like, the armory is reassuring rather than forbidding.

The Armory is the home of the New York National Guard Combat Support Company, 2nd Battalion, 174th Infantry Regiment of the 42nd Infantry Division—The *Rainbow Division*.

SMITH OPERA HOUSE, 1894, 1931, Seneca Street

The focal point of this basically Richardsonian building is a great stone arch now hidden by the present marquee and sheathing. Five recessed arches with terra-cotta decorations enclosing arched and round windows occupy the bulk of the facade. Bay windows of these are topped by balustrades. The roof line balustrade with large keystone edifice is a touch of 2nd Renaissance Revival.

The interior was remodeled in 1931 in the baroque Renaissance style with rope mold columns and gold and silver leaf, broken pediments with classical statues and urns, and a sky-blue ceiling with twinkling stars.

Itzhak Perlman and other musicians have noted the auditorium's remarkable acoustics.

Stick 1860-1890

The Stick style was a forerunner of the Queen Anne house. The idea was to emphasize with outer trim the basic structure of the building; however, this trim was actually purely decorative and took the form of vertical, horizontal, and even diagonal lines. Very steeply pitched gabled roofs added to the general impression of verticality. If there was a tower, it was asymmetrically placed and also capped with an extremely steep roof.

← THORNE-CATCHPOLE HOUSE, 1881, 9 Genesee Park

The extreme verticality of this house is self evident. The trim outlines the basic structure with the "picket fence" design spread between the bases of the principal gable. Diagonal trim intersects the gable line creating more triangles. The narrow tall tower ends in a precipitously pitched roof. The house is a fine example of the perpendicular Eastern Stick style.

Queen Anne 1880-1910

The Queen Anne house has little to do with Queen Anne (1702-1714), but this style was so named by English architects led by Richard Norman Shaw and it spread rapidly to the United States. The chief characteristic of Queen Anne houses is irregularity—steeply pitched irregular roofs with a front facing gable, bay windows, large curved glass windows, porches with much spindle work which curls around parts of the house, shingles of various textures, towers asymmetrically placed, overhangs, and a frequently bewildering array of other architectural interruptions shows the typical aversion to smooth wall surfaces of any kind of formal symmetry. Large or small, the Queen Anne house defines informality.

HUBBARD HOUSE, 1890, 65 Genesee Street
  The large round tower with conical top placed at a front facade corner dominates this exuberant house. A dentil molding and decorative banding form the cornice of the tower. Below this a string of windows with transoms creates a brilliant tower room. A double windowed dormer pierces the front gable with a triangular bay below. The front porch shows a pediment with free classical decoration. The porch roof is supported by groups of columns on a rusticated stone base. Side porches, with one recessed over the other, also have groups of columns. The aesthetic pattern of this house is of large spaces enclosed in a highly irregular, asymmetrical frame.

SPENGLER HOUSE, 1900, 236 Washington Street
The tower with its curved glass windows is topped by a steep roof and heavy decorative cornice and its placement emphasizes the basically irregular shape of the house. A two-story bay interrupts the side of the house. Dormer windows in pairs show slightly flared eaves. An oval window is an idiosyncratic touch. The porch is unexpectedly rather classic with Roman Ionic columns with volutes at 45° angles.

HALLENBECK HOUSE, 1893, 3 North Genesee Street
  The steeply pitched roof of irregular shape with slightly lower front gables establishes the basic irregular shape which delineates the Queen Anne house. The roof has slightly flared eaves and a conical dormer window. The front gable shows a triple window emphasized by a strong horizontal pediment. The porch is supported by grouped columns on pedestals. Curved windows are accentuated by slight structural overhangs. The soaring stone chimney accentuates the height of the house. Finials top the gables.

20th Century Innovations and Revivals

The early 20th Century saw both the creation of new styles such as Prairie and revivals of various periods of the past: Jacobean, Tudor, Colonial, Neo-Georgian, Neo-Classical and others. The most widely built house was the ubiquitous "bungalow" which spread from California like a plague across the land. 1900 to 1940 has been called "the most eclectic architectural period in United States history."

ST. STEPHEN'S CHURCH, 1910-1912, 56 Pulteney Street

This splendid example of the Neo-Gothic mode is dominated by a great Gothic stained glass window on the front, framed by two towers with lancet windows at the top. The solid masonry construction is composed of random-coursed rough cut limestone with arches and trim of litholite. The side walls are supported by perpendicular buttresses. The immense red tile roof, which is the striking feature when viewed from the side, establishes the warmth and feeling of Mediterranean Gothic. The interior with its many Gothic arches and beamed roof is a paradigm of restrained ecclesiastical richness.

The architects, Gordon and Madden, were meticulously guided and supervised by the pastor of the church, the Reverend Stephen V. McPadden (1872-1924). The church is a monument embracing his aesthetic ideas and the result of his study.

Jacobean 1890-1940

The Jacobean style derived its name from the reign of King James I (1603-1625). The easiest identifiable feature of the style is the high, important parapeted gable in the rather flamboyant Flemish shape. Add to this prominent chimneys, rounded arch entryways, slate roofs, and multiple window areas and handsome as well as functional buildings result. The solid masonry construction was usually of "over-burned" Harvard brick with quantities of white stone trim of doors and windows.

← COXE HALL, 1900, HOBART COLLEGE
Named for Bishop Arthur Cleveland Coxe (1818-1896), this structure has two large wings with high Flemish gables flanking the center of the building which houses administration offices, class rooms, and theater. The fronts of the wings have two-story three-sided bays of white stone. The center section has a recessed entrance with three round stone arches. The cornice line of the entry shows a Renaissance balustrade. The large square tower, asymmetrically placed, is finished with crenelations. The wing on the right, designed later by I. Edgar Hill, has two front-facing parapeted Flemish gables. The principal masonry is "over-burned" Harvard brick with integral white stone and trim.
Architects: Clinton and Russell, New York City

← MEDBERY HALL, 1900, HOBART COLLEGE
This dormitory has a pavilion at both ends and in the center with high parapeted Flemish gables. Doorways are rounded arches of white stone. Windows also have white stone surrounds which strongly contrast with the "over-burned" Harvard brick. Six great chimneys tower over the slate roof. The interior arrangements consist of a series of two-room suites of living room and bedroom. The Jacobean style proved eminently adaptable to the function of the building.
Architects: Clinton and Russell, New York City.

▲ BRENNAN HOUSE, 1924, 720 South Main Street

Five intersecting gables of varying size establish the character of this house. Brick, stone, and slate are the construction materials. Strings of two and three leaded windows add to the general asymmetrical effect. Sills and lintels are of white stone. A great chimney on the front punctuates the silhouette of the building. The main door is rounded Jacobean with white stone surround. The aesthetic effect is charm and livability.

▼ GRANT HOUSE, 1923, 816 South Main Street

The gables of this house are parapeted with gray sandstone. Banks of three and four windows have leaded panes. The main door is a Tudor arch of gray stone. A steep pitched roof of slate completes this house of brick and stone.

Tudor 1890-1940

Named for the Tudor sovereigns of England from Henry VII to Elizabeth I (1485-1603), the Tudor style is based more on the earlier designs of this period rather than the later more effulgent Elizabethan constructions.

Multiple gables often intersecting each other, steep roofs of expensive slate, banks of multiple windows grouped into strings of three or more, window surrounds of cast stone, and prominent chimneys asymmetrically placed are the notable characteristics of the style. Walls may be of stone, brick, or smooth stucco with distinctive "Tudor" half-timbering in varying patterns depending on the whim of the architect. Main entrances are either rounded in the Jacobean manner or show the flattened Tudor arch.

Good Tudor houses are architect designed, expensive, and of landmark status. The aesthetic effect is of an enlarged cottage or manor house that is still cozy and liveable.

ST. STEPHEN'S RECTORY, 1912, 84 Pulteney Street

This splendid example of the Tudor style is notable for its half-timbering on smooth stucco. The Gothic pointed arch doorway is centered at the base of a large gable. Bands of windows from two to seven are surrounded by white stone. A large outer chimney is centered in one gable end. Wall dormer windows with peaked timbering project into the slate roof. The house exemplifies both taste and warmth.

Prairie 1900-1920

Developed by a group of Chicago architects of whom Frank Lloyd Wright became the most famous, the Prairie style was a truly independent American style not derived from English or European sources. The usual emphasis is on horizontal lines furthered by a low hipped roof with wide eaves, rows of windows, and contrasting linear colors. In addition to the elongated rectangular house a more "boxy" type was developed which still tried to maintain a strong horizontal look.

PAGE HOUSE, 1914, 380 Washington Street
   The strong horizontal lines of this house make it a splendid example of the Prairie style. Contrasting colors accentuate the effect. A very low hipped roof and wide flat eaves over both first and second stories parallel the flatness of its setting. A simple slab is cantilevered over a low porch with solid rectangular rails and flattened round flower pots. Banks of large-paned windows fill the facade. The house strongly suggests the animating spirit of Frank Lloyd Wright.

WHITE SPRINGS MANOR, 1898, White Springs Lane

As an example of Neo-Georgian pomp, this mansion is outstanding. Four Ionic columns with volutes at 45° angles support a large pediment with semi-elliptical fanlight. Ionic pilasters with similar volutes enhance the impressiveness of the facade and add to the importance of the encircling entablature. The main door has a heavy "surround" of transom and side lights. Over the door is a balcony with door and Adamesque fanlight. Two large recessed wings enlarge the house. Dormer windows are crowned with classical pediments. The geographic setting of this house on a high ridge overlooking Seneca Lake and two counties provides a spectacular view commensurate with the grandeur of the house.

MEANS-WELCH HOUSE, 1908, 454 Castle Street
   The elements of the Neo-Classical style are evidenced in this house which has a full-length portico of four Ionic colunms, an entablature and pediment outlined in dentil molding, and a fanlight window centered in the pediment. The door with transom and side lights is derived from the Greek Revival. The triple and double windows are an atypical feature not found in original classic architecture.

HOSKINS HOUSE, 1907, 527 South Main Street

This Colonial Revival house has a side gabled roof with symmetrically placed chimneys. The Adamesque front door is accentuated with a front porch extended forward and supported by slender columns. The porch ceiling has a curved underside to match the fanlight over the door. The windows have sashes of six panes each. The triple window over the porch is a variant from original colonials. Two Ionic pilasters at the front corners emphasize the house's classicality.

Architect: Claude Bragdon, Rochester, New York

UNITED STATES POST OFFICE, 1906, 67 Castle Street
  Stong Roman Doric columns support an impressive entablature with a frieze of triglyphs and metopes which encircles the building. Heavy dentil molding lines the roof line as well as the encircling entablature. The centered Roman arch doorway is flanked by two windows of the same dimension on either side. All have three white keystones highlighting the arches. Over the windows are white stone panels with bas-reliefs depicting industry, education, aviation, agriculture, and an American eagle over the main door. These were designed and carved by Works Progress Administration artists and installed in 1938. The Post Office is a fine example of academic classical architecture.

NESTER VILLA, 1909-1914, 1001 Lochland Road

Byron M. Nester (1884-1947), a native Genevan and a gifted amateur artist, designer, and aesthete, built this Italian Renaissance villa after an extensive trip to Italy. In its location on a bluff overlooking Seneca Lake it emulates the settings of villas on Lake Garda and Lake Maggiore in Northern Italy.

LAKE FRONT

The lake front shows a center section of three arched Palladian windows in the second story. A classical pediment frames the double door entry. Balustrades top the first and third stories. Pilasters on the second and third floors of the center wing, and stone quoins at the corners emphasize the verticality of the facade. Niches with classical busts ornament the wings. A low-pitched hip roof of red tiles completes the villa with a strong horizontal line.

STREET FRONT
A giant Palladian arched porte-cochère with Roman Ionic columns centers the street front. The interior of this villa is thoroughly Renaissance. Marble columns in the entry vestibule, elaborate coffered ceilings, and hand carved massive stone chimney pieces from Italy complete this beautifully designed example of academic historicity.

The historical prototype of this building is the Lancelloti Villa in Frascati in the Alban Hills outside of Rome.

GAS STATION, 1929, Main Street
Constructed in the Art Moderne manner of smooth cement, this station shows the lingering influence of the Greek Revival and the classical heritage of Geneva. Demilune in shape, ten simple sturdy columns support an unadorned heavy entablature. The edifice reveals how classical elements can be adapted for a commercial enterprise.